My Sister
My Friend

Artwork by For Giving Souls

HARVEST HOUSE PUBLISHERS

EUGENE, OREGON

My Sister, My Friend

Text Copyright © 2005 by Harvest House Publishers
Eugene, Oregon 97402

ISBN-13: 978-0-7369-1518-2
ISBN-10: 0-7369-1518-4

For Giving Souls™ © 2005 by G Studios, LLC. For Giving Souls
Trademarks owned by G Studios, LLC, Newport Beach, CA USA and
used by Harvest House Publishers, Inc., under authorization. For more
information regarding art prints featured in this book, please contact:

>   G Studios, LLC
>   4500 Campus Drive, Suite 200
>   Newport Beach, CA 92660
>   949.261.1300
>   www.gstudiosllc.com

Design and production by Garborg Design Works, Minneapolis,
Minnesota

Printed in China

05 06 07 08 09 10 11 12 / LP / 10 9 8 7 6 5 4 3 2 1

To My Sister,

BETTY

With Love,

DORIS   - _2005_

A sister is a gift to the heart,
A friend to the spirit,
A golden thread to the meaning of life.

ISADORA JAMES

A ministering angel

For there is no friend like a sister;
In calm or stormy weather;
To cheer one on the tedious way,
To fetch one if one goes astray,
To lift one if one totters down,
To strengthen whilst one stands.

CHRISTINA ROSSETTI

We are more than just acquaintances...it's as
if we are cut from the same fabric. Even though
we appear to be sewn in a different
pattern, we have a common thread that
won't be broken— by people or years or distance.

AUTHOR UNKNOWN

shall my sister be.

WILLIAM SHAKESPEARE

Sisters are for sharing

Both within the family and
without, our sisters hold
up our mirrors: our images
of who we are and of
who we can dare to become.

ELIZABETH FISHEL

Then come, my Sister!
come, I pray,
With speed put on
your woodland dress;
And bring no book:
for this one day
We'll give to idleness.

WILLIAM WORDSWORTH
To My Sister

laughter and wiping tears.

AUTHOR UNKNOWN

With a sister by your side, you can
always count on someone who knew you
as you were and loves you as you are.

AUTHOR UNKNOWN

Sisters touch your heart in ways no other
could. Sisters share...their hopes, their fears,
their love, everything they have. Real
friendship springs from their special bonds.

CARRIE BAGWELL

Is solace anywhere more comforting

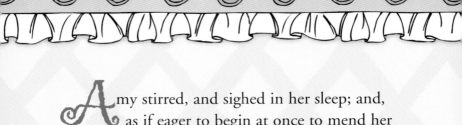

*A*my stirred, and sighed in her sleep; and, as if eager to begin at once to mend her fault, Jo looked up with an expression on her face which it had never worn before.

"I let the sun go down on my anger; I wouldn't forgive her, and today, if it hadn't been for Laurie, it might have been too late! How could I be so wicked?" said Jo, half aloud, as she leaned over her sister, softly stroking the wet hair scattered on the pillow.

As if she heard, Amy opened her eyes, and held out her arms, with a smile that went straight to Jo's heart. Neither said a word, but they hugged one another close, in spite of the blankets, and everything was forgiven and forgotten in one hearty kiss.

LOUISA MAY ALCOTT
Little Women

than in the arms of a sister?
ALICE WALKER

Chance made us sisters,

Sisters are special
From young ones to old.
God gave me a sister
More precious than gold.

AUTHOR UNKNOWN

Sisters share a closeness no one else can understand...
A sister's always there to give a hug or lend a hand.
Sisters are the best friends in the whole wide world, it's true...
And that friendship is a blessing that lasts a lifetime through.

AUTHOR UNKNOWN

hearts made us friends.

AUTHOR UNKNOWN

Sisters make the real
conversations...not the saying but the
never needing to say is what counts.

MARGARET LEE RUNBECK

There was once a child, and he strolled about a good deal, and thought of a number of things. He had a sister, who was a child, too, and his constant companion. These two used to wonder all day long. They wondered at the beauty of the flowers; they wondered at the height and blueness of the sky; they wondered at the depth of the bright water; they wondered at the goodness and the power of God who made the lovely world.

CHARLES DICKENS
A Child's Dream of a Star

A sister's a friend who brings laughter your way,
She supports you in all that you do,
She's been at the heart of so many glad moments
And shares precious memories with you…
She knows how you've changed,
How you've grown through the years,
And she knows all that you're dreaming of,
She's the comfort of family, the warm touch of home…
She's the beautiful blessing of love.

Many women do noble things,

When Morning comes with smiles so gay,
O'er heathy hills I love to stray,
Where lustrous drops of pearly dew
Sparkle upon the hare-bell blue,
And bathe the thymy cover'd ground,
Whence sweetest fragrance steals around.
Ah, Anna! then, to friendship true,
I think of moments past—and you!

MISS S. EVANCE

but you surpass them all.

THE BOOK OF PROVERBS

The day God blessed us with you,
Was truly a gift to us all.
He gave me someone
Who He knew would
Always love me,
Someone I could talk to,
Share my life with,
Laugh with at all times,
Especially when I needed it most.
What God gave me was you!
My sister...my best friend.

DANA LYNN

The desire to be and have a sister is a primitive and profound one that may have everything or nothing to do with the family a woman is born to. It is a desire to know and be known by someone who shares blood and body, history and dreams . . .

ELIZABETH FISHEL

I don't see how you can write and act such splendid things, Jo. You're a regular Shakespeare!" exclaimed Beth, who firmly believed that her sisters were gifted with wonderful genius in all things. In spite of her small vanities, Margaret had a sweet and pious nature, which unconsciously influenced her sisters, especially Jo, who loved her very tenderly, and obeyed her because her advice was so gently given. The two older girls were a great deal to one another, but each took one of the younger sisters into her keeping and watched over her in her own way, "playing mother" they called it, and put their sisters in the places of discarded dolls with the maternal instinct of little women.

LOUISA MAY ALCOTT
Little Women

The sister bond is often greater than

that with a friend or brother...

Dr. Harriette McAdoo

"My dear Jane!" exclaimed Elizabeth,
"you are too good. Your sweetness and
disinterestedness are really angelic;
I do not know what to say to you.
I feel as if I have never done you
justice, or loved you as you deserve."

JANE AUSTEN
Pride and Prejudice

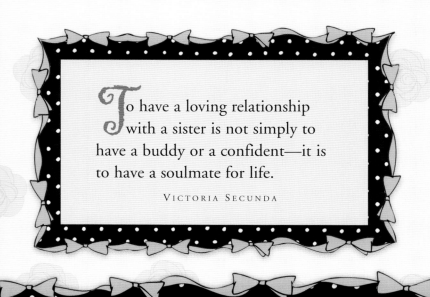

To have a loving relationship
with a sister is not simply to
have a buddy or a confident—it is
to have a soulmate for life.

VICTORIA SECUNDA

Sisters don't need words. They have
perfected a language of snarls and
smiles and frowns and winks...
expressions of shocked surprise and
incredulity and disbelief. Sniffs
and snorts and gasps and sighs...that
can undermine any tale you're telling.

PAM BROWN

My sister shares a part of me...
that no one else shall ever see.
And when the days and miles divide us...
the bond we have will live inside us.
Together sharing dreams, love, and laughter...
My sister for always, my friend...forever.

AUTHOR UNKNOWN

We have shared each other's gladness

and wept each other's tears.

<small>CHARLES JEFFREY</small>

You don't choose your family. They are God's gift to you, as you are to them.

DESMOND TUTU

For many years we've shared our lives
One roof we once lived under
Sometimes we laughed, sometimes we cried
Through winter storms and thunder
The younger years have faded fast
We've gone our separate ways
But through all time our friendship lasts
Our bond in life remains
As summer brings the happy times
The autumn winds will whisper
A closer friend I'd never find
Than the one I call my Sister.

AUTHOR UNKNOWN

What greater thing is there for
human souls than to feel that they
are joined for life—to be with each other
in silent, unspeakable memories.

GEORGE ELIOT

A sister is a little bit of

tears

Sisters—they share the agony and the exhilaration. As youngsters they may share popsicles, chewing gum, hair dryers, and bedrooms. When they grow up, they share confidences, careers and children, and some even chat for hours every day.

ROXANNE BROWN

childhood that can never be lost.

MARION C. GARRETTY

She is your mirror, shining back at you with a
world of possibilities. She is your witness, who
sees you at your worst and best, and loves you
anyway. She is your partner in crime, your mid-
night companion, someone who knows when you
are smiling, even in the dark. She is your
teacher, your defense attorney, your personal
press agent, even your shrink. Some days, she's
the reason you wish you were an only child.

BARBARA ALPERT

Having a sister is like having a best
friend you can't get rid of. You know
whatever you do, they'll still be there.

AMY LI

With so much that separates us in
this world, it is comforting to
remember that there are certain similarities
we all share, universal sentiments and
experiences that continually bind us
together as one family.

MARGARET BECKER

My sisters have

GEORGE WASSERSTEIN

taught me how to live.

what one loves in childhood

*P*lease, God, let me have a baby sister…I repeated it over and over like that, the way I heard people at church do, under my breath, kind of like a whisper. It seemed like forever before the phone rang, but when it did, we all jumped. Aunt Sophie knocked the handset off the wall as she ran to get it. She seemed scared.

"Hello?" Her voice was shaky. "Yes…*really!* Oh, thank God! How long? Uh-huh. How big?"

My insides were spinning. *Please, God, let me have a baby sister…Please, God, let me have a baby sister…*

Aunt Sophie hung up the receiver and spun around just in time to see Joey sticking his tongue out at the phone. I was glad for it, too, because he was finally going to get it! But Aunt Sophie didn't seem to notice.

"Kids, go get washed up. We're going down to the hospital to see your new baby sister!"

My new baby sister? It worked!

MARGARET BECKER
Growing Up Together

stays in the heart forever.
MARY JO PUTNEY

We shared many secrets, the same mom and dad,
We shared lots of good times, don't think of the bad.
Our memories we'll cherish, with love without end,
I'm glad you're my sister, I'm glad you're my friend.

AUTHOR UNKNOWN